Doves As Pets

Facts & Information

Breeding, Diet, Housing, Health,
Where to Buy, Raising, and More.

By Lolly Brown

Copyrights and Trademarks

All rights reserved. No part of this book may be reproduced or transformed in any form or by any means, graphic, electronic, or mechanical, including photocopying, recording, taping, or by any information storage retrieval system, without the written permission of the author.

This publication is Copyright ©2015 NRB Publishing, an imprint of Pack & Post Plus, LLC. Nevada. All products, graphics, publications, software and services mentioned and recommended in this publication are protected by trademarks. In such instance, all trademarks & copyright belong to the respective owners. For information consult www.NRBpublishing.com

Disclaimer and Legal Notice

This product is not legal, medical, or accounting advice and should not be interpreted in that manner. You need to do your own due-diligence to determine if the content of this product is right for you. While every attempt has been made to verify the information shared in this publication, neither the author, neither publisher, nor the affiliates assume any responsibility for errors, omissions or contrary interpretation of the subject matter herein. Any perceived slights to any specific person(s) or organization(s) are purely unintentional.

We have no control over the nature, content and availability of the web sites listed in this book. The inclusion of any web site links does not necessarily imply a recommendation or endorse the views expressed within them. We take no responsibility for, and will not be liable for, the websites being temporarily unavailable or being removed from the internet.

The accuracy and completeness of information provided herein and opinions stated herein are not guaranteed or warranted to produce any particular results, and the advice and strategies, contained herein may not be suitable for every individual. Neither the author nor the publisher shall be liable for any loss incurred as a consequence of the use and application, directly or indirectly, of any information presented in this work. This publication is designed to provide information in regard to the subject matter covered.

Neither the author nor the publisher assume any responsibility for any errors or omissions, nor do they represent or warrant that the ideas, information, actions, plans, suggestions contained in this book is in all cases accurate. It is the reader's responsibility to find advice before putting anything written in this book into practice. The information in this book is not intended to serve as legal, medical, or accounting advice.

Foreword

When I first became acquainted with companion doves, I remember having the clear thought, "How boring!" Doves are so gentle by nature and so content to be what they are, happily settled into their cages and bonded for life with their mates, that I couldn't imagine these birds being particularly interesting pets.

That was a totally erroneous assumption on my part and one I have since abandoned completely. Being in the world in a peaceful way as doves tend to live their lives does not mean that they are not engaged with what is going on around them. I have discovered that doves are not only highly intelligent they are also keen observers.

Doves thrive on constancy and routine and require a real connection with their human keepers even if the birds are living as a mated pair. I was also surprised to discover that a dove's need to mate is so strong they have no particular gender preference. It is quite common to see same gender, dove couples that are completely devoted to one another.

When compared to other potential companion birds, doves have the great advantage of being soft voiced. I assure you that the various parrot types will cheerfully raise the roof when they're not happy about something. A dove may, at most, rattle around his cage and give his seed cup a good shake.

While doves are susceptible to the effects of stress and require a managed environment, they are, otherwise, simple birds to maintain as you will see in the chapter on husbandry and care.

The greatest initial expense is in acquiring a cage that is large enough for a pair of doves to spread their wings and get move freely about. Although doves are primarily sedentary, the perches in their habitat provide vital exercise for the birds' feet.

My advice to any bird owner is always to buy the largest cage you can afford and place in your home. The best choice for doves is a "flight" cage (often called an aviary or cockatiel cage.)

You must also be prepared for the need to clean your doves' cage daily. This is not only necessary maintenance for the health of your birds, but also an important precaution for your own welfare.

Humans may contract many of the diseases from which doves and other birds can suffer. Excellent husbandry practices are the best means of prevention.

If I were to make any overriding caution, however, to a person considering adopting a dove or doves (and I do recommend keeping a mated pair) it would be to consider the longevity of these birds. A well cared for dove can live to be 20 years of age!

Unless you are willing (and happy) to make a commitment to a dove for the duration of its life, do not even consider an adoption.

If, however, you are thrilled by the prospect of forging a relationship with an intelligent and affectionate bird that will be with you for up to two decades, you may have just found your perfect match!

Acknowledgments

I would like to express my gratitude towards my family, friends, and colleagues for their kind co-operation and encouragement which helped me in completion of this book.

I would like to express my special gratitude and thanks to my loving husband for his patience, understanding, and support.

My thanks and appreciations also go to my colleagues and people who have willingly helped me out with their abilities.

Additional thanks to my children, whose love and care for our family pets inspired me to write this book.

Table of Contents

Table of Contents

Chapter 1 - Introducing the Dove

As pets, doves are valued not only for their mellow, peaceful nature, but also for their longevity. With proper care, it's possible for a dove to live as long as 20 years.

The birds thrive when kept in pairs and are both social and smart. Although quiet, they have loving personalities and tend to bond closely with their humans.

History of Man and the Dove

The dove is one of mankind's most ubiquitous symbols, regarded around the world as a harbinger of peace, safety, and serenity. They are often seen as messengers and are associated with:

- motherhood

- love and grace
- promises made
- devotion
- divinity and holiness
- sacrifice
- ascension
- purification
- hope

Geographically, doves are found on every continent except Antarctica and in every region except the most arid parts of the Sahara Desert.

Metaphorically, doves inhabit the pages of the world's great religious texts and are often seen as a holy symbol. It was a dove, for instance, that signaled Noah that the waters of the Great Flood had begun to recede. The Christian Holy Spirit is often depicted as a descending dove.

Both doves and pigeons are members of the *Columbidae* family, which includes 310 species. Of these, the largest member is the Crowned Pigeon, a native of New Guinea, that weighs 4.4-8.8 lbs. / 2-4 kg.

The smallest member is the Ground Dove, which is roughly the size of a common house sparrow and weighs a scant 22 grams.

In terms of general physical characteristics, members of the *Columbidae* family have:

- short bills

- short legs
- small heads (which they bob to improve their vision)
- large, compact bodies
- large wings capable of strong flight and maneuverability

In many parts of the world, the terms "dove" and "pigeon" are used interchangeably, and scientifically there really is no difference in the two birds.

Typically, the word "pigeon" refers to the larger *Columbidae* species, while doves are smaller birds.

Overall, doves are docile creatures. They are easy to keep as companion birds, and in fact the care instructions for both doves and pigeons are essentially identical. Both types of *Columbidae* have enjoyed a close relationship with mankind since ancient times.

Types of Doves

Although there are more than 300 species of *Columbidae*, only five types of doves are routinely sought by enthusiasts to live as pets. Within these five species, however, especially in the world of show doves, there is great diversity.

In the broadest terms, doves fall into two major groups, fruit eaters (mainly kept in zoos and by serious hobbyists) and seed eaters.

Seed eaters are said to be granivorous, while the fruit eaters are frugivorus. The first group tends to feed on seed found on the ground, while the fruit eaters feed in trees.

In addition, many ground doves also consume insects, snails, and worms, and some fruit doves will even eat small reptiles.

Ring Neck or Barbaray Dove

The hardy Ring Neck Dove, *Streptopelia capicola*, domesticated from a species indigenous to Africa, comes in more than 40 color mutations. These are the primary doves shown in competitive exhibits.

(Note that you will see also see these birds referred to as Ringed-Neck Doves.)

All Ring Neck doves have a partial collar of feathers at the nape of the neck. On the wild birds this collar is black, but shades vary within cultivated color mutations.

Since they depend on surface water for hydration, feral Ring Neck doves gather in large flocks near bodies of water to drink and to bathe. Their primary social relationship, however, is with a bonded mate.

The wild Ring Neck dove is dark on the upper side in tones of gray and brown with lavender at the nape of the neck turning pinking below and blending into a white lower belly. Individual plumage varies greatly. Overall these birds measure 9.8-10.4 inches / 25-26.5 cm in length.

There are six types of Ring Neck dove from which all color mutations have been developed:

- *Streptopelia capicola capicola* found in southwestern South Africa
- *Streptopelia capicola abunda* found in central South Africa
- *Streptopelia capicola damarensis* found in the arid interior of southern Africa
- *Streptopelia capicola onguati* indigenous to western Nambia and Angola
- *Streptopelia capicola tropica* native to the tropical and sub-tropical woodlands from South Africa to the South Sudan
- *Streptopelia capicola somalica* living from northern Tanzania to Somalia and Ethiopia

Ring Neck doves are often confused with the Barbary dove, Eurasian collared dove, Vinaceous dove, Red-eyed dove, Red turtledove, and Mourning collared dove.

The Ring Neck doves kept as companions are primarily the descendants of other captive birds and are the product of planned breeding programs.

With no exceptional housing requirements beyond adequate space, and known for the ease with which they are bred, Ring Neck doves are also highly popular as companion birds.

Ring Neck doves are often found in pet shops, and are distinguished from other species by their prominent neck

ring. Their lifespan in captivity is approximately 20 years.
Diamond Dove

The Diamond Dove, *Geopelia cuneata*, is native to Australia.
A small and popular creature, the Diamond Dove can be
found in approximately a dozen color varieties and is also
widely used as a show animal in competition.

They are smaller birds, measuring no more than 9-11 inches
/ 19-21 cm in length. The wild form has white spots or
diamonds on the wings, which are edged in black. Their
eyes are orange and encircled by a red eye ring.

Wild Diamond Doves are light blue-grey on the head, neck,
and breast, with a creamy abdomen and brown-gray
coloration on the back and tail. The legs and feet are pink
and the bill is dark grey.

They are seen most often on the ground in pairs or small feeding groups, taking seeds from grass and eating ants. Diamond Doves have a variety of calls that are slow, soft, mournful and may rise to a pleasing falsetto tone.

Larger inhabitants of an aviary can bully Diamond Doves, but otherwise the species is an easy bird to breed and to keep. They do spend a large amount of time on the ground and should not be kept in cages with wire bottoms, which can seriously injure their feet.

Diamond Doves require smaller seed mixes like those prepared for finch and canary species and should also be given vegetables and greens.

Since the birds swallow seeds whole, they need to be supplied with grit to aid with digestion. Like all doves, they also have a high need for companionship and will do best when kept in pairs.

Their lifespan is even longer than that of the Ring Neck dove. Diamond Doves can live to the ripe old age of 25 in captivity!

Mourning Dove

The Mourning Dove, *Zenaida macroura,* has a sad, almost melancholy call or "coo." It is native to North and South America, and is a placid and peaceful creature.

You may also see this dove referred to as a Wood Dove, Turtledove, American Mourning Dove, Rain Dove,

Carolina Pigeon, or Carolina Turtledove.

Their bodies are a muted light grey and brown. On average Mourning Doves are 12 inches / 31 cm in length and weigh 4.0-6 ounces / 112-170 grams. They are slender with a short, dark bill and short, reddish legs. In flight, their wings are broad and elliptical and their tails are long and tapered.

The five sub-species of Mourning Dove are:

- *Zenaida macroura carolinensis* – found in the eastern parts of North America
- *Zenaida macroura clarionensis* – Clarion Island
- *Zenaida macroura macroura* – West Indian
- *Zenaida macroura marginella* – found in the western parts of North America
- *Zenaida macroura turturilla* – native to Panama

There is overlap in the ranges of most of these sub-species making it difficult to pin down their geographic ranges with any precision. In total, the birds are distributed over 4,200,000 square miles / 11,000,000 km².

Spotted Dove or Laceneck Dove

Sometimes called a Chinese Turtle Dove or Spotted Turtle Dove, *Streptopelia chinensis*, is another hardy species that lives peacefully with other doves unless it is crowded. This reaction can be a husbandry issue during mating and nesting seasons.

The species is native to Indian and Southeast Asia, but has been introduced around the world. They are buff brown birds with black collars spotted in white and long tails. Specimens range in length from 11.2-12.8 inches / 28-32 cm.

The Rock Dove

The Rock Dove, *Columba livia*, is an excellent beginning bird although it is actually the common feral "pigeon." Like many pigeons, Rock Doves have a homing instinct, so they can be allowed out of their coop for free flight time. They will return in the evening and are, overall, extremely simple to keep.

Wild specimens are pale gray birds with black double wing bars. Since this bird is technically considered a pigeon, you will find that they, too, have been widely cultivated in planned breeding programs for unique colorations and plumage.

The pigeon fancy is even more active than the dove fancy and includes enthusiasts who competitively race their birds. The contestants are taken to a remote location and released with their return flight timed against other birds in the race.

Adult Rock Doves are 11-15 inches / 29-37 cm in length with a wingspan of 24-28 inches / 62-72 cm and a body weight of 8.4-13.4 ounces / 238-380 grams.

Doves Shown in Competition

Like all enthusiast cultures, there are dove associations and clubs around the world. Members not only share their love for the birds and actively work for their welfare, many enter their doves in organized competitions.

In the United States, the American Dove Association (ADA) sponsors dove shows throughout the years with the most important being the National Young Bird Show held in Louisville, Kentucky each October. Both Ring Neck and Diamond Doves are allowed in ADA shows.

Internationally, you can check the listings of the International Dove Society for events, breeder listings, and other useful information. See:

www.internationaldovesociety.com.

Ring Neck Dove Colors

With more than 40 color variations in Ring Neck Doves

alone, show doves are the focus of organized breeding programs that carefully cultivate desirable mutations across a range of both colors and textures.

There are also three recognized plumage variations that add a textural element to the dove's appearance:

- *Silky* - Silky doves are characterized by a special placement of the webbing of their feathers. The inner web of the feather connects to the shaft, but the outer web does not. This uneven placement creates a "silky" or "rippled" texture in the plumage. This effect is seen over the bird's entire body.

- *Tufted* - The tuft on a dove will vary from bird to bird from a mere "bump" to an actual upright tuft. It is a mutation that can be produced in any Ring Neck Dove color variation. Essentially, the tuft looks like a "cowlick."

- *Crested* - The crest on a dove's head appears at the back of the head as a sort of "upsweep." It almost seems as if the bird has a case of "bed head." The size and shape will vary by individual dove.

The following list describes some of the many color combinations seen in Ring Neck Doves. For the most part, show classes are organized by color so that like birds compete.

- *Albino* - Body, tail, and head that are completely white. There is no visible neck ring and the eyes are bright pink.
- *Apricot* - The body color varies from white to cream with a pinkish-orange hue on the wings, back, and tail. The head, neck, and breast are pure white as is the neck ring and flight feathers. The reddish eyes have a mottled iris.

- *Light Ash* - A dove with a white or extremely diluted gray body. The color on the head, neck, and breast is a rich almond with some similar penciling on the back and shoulders. The neck ring is gray or white and the bill should be a light color. The eyes are red-brown. The primary and secondary flight feathers and tail feathers are white to silvery gray.

- *Bull-Eye White* - A dove with a white head, body, wings, and tail with black eyes, no neck ring and a dark bill.

- *Cream* - The color of the cream body is similar to that

of a manila folder, with white head, breast, and flight feathers. The neck ring is a light brown and the ruby eyes have a mottled iris.

- **Cream Pied** - This dove has cream markings on a sandy, light tan body color. The head, breast, and flight feathers are white with a gray / diluted charcoal gray neck ring. The bill is dark tipped and the feet and legs are red. The eyes are ruby red.

- **Frosty** - Frosty doves have bodies that are a slate grey / blue with no violet on the head and neck and grizzling on the primary and secondary flight feathers. White may extend on to the tail feathers with patches of white on the rump, body, and head. The neck ring is black and the eyes are red. There is a bill stripe on the top or side and the legs and feet are red / purple.

- **Ivory** - An Ivory dove is light brown to gray on the body, wings and tail with an off white head, neck, and breast and a black to charcoal neck ring. The light bill has a dark tip and the eyes are mottled.

- **Fawn/Blond** - A dove with a sandy body, tail, and head and a black neck ring edged in white. The flight feathers are diluted. The bill is black and the eye is red / orange.

- **Blond Frosty** - This dove's body is a blue gray with a lighter shade on the head and breast. The tail feathers may be splotched in white and the inner web of the primary and secondary flight feathers are grizzled. The neck ring is black with white tips and the eyes are ruby red.

- *Ash* - The body of this dove is white to an extremely diluted gray. The head, neck, and breast are a rich almond and there may be almond penciling on the shoulders and back. The neck ring is gray to white.

- *Ice* - An Ice Ring Neck Dove has a white body that can only be described as "intense" in its purity. There will, however, be 1-7 blue-gray feathers randomly placed somewhere on the wings and body. The bill is dark or mottled and the eyes are also dark. There is no neck ring.

- *Blond Ivory* - A dove with a white body, wings, and head that is sometimes referred to as a "dirty" or "pearly" white. The neck ring ranges from dark gray to black.

- *Orange* - The body of this bird is a rust-peach-orange, which is also present on the head and wings. The bill is light and the neck ring is white, as are the primary flight feathers. The eye is chestnut red. This is the dilute version of the Tangerine dove.

- *Orange Chinmoy* - A dove with a white body that is marked with orange spots and an orange neck ring.

- *Orange Neck* - A dove with a white body, wing, and tail that often has almond traces on the shoulder and back. The head, neck, and breast should all show rich almond coloration and the neck ring should be white. The beak is light, but can be dark at the base. The eyes are chestnut red. In some cases there will be a white "cap" present on the head.

- *Orange Pearled* - A dove with an orange body interspersed with feathers edged or tipped in white for a pearled effect. The head is typically a lighter orange with no violet present there or on the neck and chest. The bill may range from light to dark. The neck ring and flight feathers are white. This is the dilute variation of the Tangerine Pearled dove.
- *Pink* - An extremely pale dove with a diluted red / brown cast over the body and head. The neck ring and flight feathers are white. The bird has a light bone bill and a reddish brown eye.

- *Roan* - A dove with a dull brown body and a light violet breast and head. The flight feathers and mid-feathers are frosted or grizzled and the neck ring is black. The color of the bill varies.

- *Rosy* - Rosy doves are reddish orange on the back and wing shields in a shade darker than the Peach coloration. The head, neck, and breast are all violet and the neck ring is black. The bill color is light with a dark tip or dark overall.

- *Tangerine* - This dove's body is an intense red / rusty color with a violet breast, neck and head. The flight feathers are silvery gray to white and the neck ring ranges from white to dark gray. The eyes are chestnut red.

- **Tangerine White Back** - Similar to the Tangerine Pearled. The Tangerine White Back should be white from the region of the lower neck back along the body to the tail. Both the neck ring and flight feathers are also white.

- **Violet Neck** - This dove's body, wing, and tail are white with some traces of tangerine pearling on the shoulders and back. Look for a rich violet on the head, neck, and breast with a white neck ring. The eye is chestnut red and there is sometimes a white "cap" atop the head.

- **White** - As the name suggest, this bird is solid colored in a range of "tea" to light "cream." There is the faintest suggestion of a light neck ring. The eyes are orange. White Ring Neck Doves, often referred to as "peace" doves, are the variety most often released at special events as a symbolic gesture. The harmful effects of this practice on the doves themselves will be discussed in a special section of this book, but it cannot be overstated that these creatures are not suited to survival in the wild and should not be subjected to such releases.

- **Wild** - A Wild Ring Neck Dove is dark grey to brown on the body, tail, and wing shields with light edging on the nearly black primary flight feathers. On males, the head, neck, and breast are pinkish to amethyst in color with hens showing lighter shades of the same coloration. The neck ring is black, edged in a thin line of white at the top and bottom. The eyes are red chestnut and the feet are red / purple.

Diamond Dove Colors

Some popular colorations see in Diamond Doves include the following:

- *Blue* - Blue Diamond Doves are brown on the back and shoulders, which are marked with white spots or "diamonds." The head, neck, and breast are silver while the tail is brown and tipped in black. The underside is white over pink feet. The bill is black and the eyes are bright red.

- *Blue Pied* - The Blue Pied Diamond Dove is brown on the back, shoulders, wing, and tail, but can have white feathers anywhere on the body. The most likely locations are the head, neck, and breast. The eyes are ruby red encircled by a bright red eye ring. The bill is black and the primary flight feathers are a rich mahogany tipped in black.

- *Blue White Rump* - This dove is steel blue on the back and shoulders where the characteristic diamond spots occur. The color lightens to silver blue on the neck and breast, while the back and tail are white with intermingled gray-brown feathers. The underside is white. A red eye ring encircles the ruby eye and the bill is gray.

- *Blue White Tail* - The Blue White Tail is similar to the Blue White Rump with the primary difference being the snow white back and tail on this animal in contrast to the steel blue of the shoulders and wings where the diamond spots occur. The feathers on the neck, head, and breast are blue gray and the underside is white.

- *Brilliant* - A Brilliant Diamond Dove is light beige over the whole body with a white underside. The bill is silver to beige and the eyes are red with a large red eye ring. The wings are extremely dilute and appear as a pale beige with lighter tips.

- *Brilliant White Tail* - The Brilliant White Tail is a rare coloration in Diamond Doves and exceptionally beautiful. The dove appears to be almost snow white, but is a lovely light beige on the head, neck, and breast and extending over the shoulders and wings. The eyes are red and encircled by a red eye ring. The bill is light beige.

- *Cinnamon* - The Cinnamon color is the most basic of the reds among Diamond Doves, with all other red mutations originating from this bird. The shade is deep rust on the shoulders and wings while the tail and back are brown and the head, neck, and breast silver gray. The underside is white. A bright red eye ring surrounds the ruby eye. The bill is black to gray.

- *Peach* - The Peach Diamond Dove shows a faded yellow color on the head and neck extending down over the shoulders, back, wings, and tail as well as on the breast. The underside is white. The eyes may be ruby red to yellow-orange and are encircled by a red-orange eye ring. The bill is light beige.

- *Red* – Red Diamond Doves should more accurately be described as rusty in coloration. Males, however, have less rust and more silver on their backs whereas females are heavily rusted on the back, shoulders, and wings.

- *Silver* - The Silver Diamond dove is silver on the shoulders, wings, back, and tail while the head, neck, and breast are a pale gray. The underside is white. A red orange eye ring encircles the ruby red eyes flanking the silver bill.

- *Silver White Tail* - This dove is very light in color and appears almost completely white until they darken with age. They are much brighter as adults than a Brilliant, showing a lovely light silver on the shoulders, lower back, rump, and tail while the head, neck, and breast remain white.

- *Ultimate Red* - The Ultimate Red Diamond Dove varies in coloration by gender. Males are off-white on the head, neck, breast, shoulder, and wings with white on the tail and back and a white underside. Females are intensely colored with bright rust red on the shoulders, back, and wings. Their heads are light rust, while the neck and breast are light gray and the underside is white. A small red eye ring encircles the ruby eyes.

- *Yellow* - The Yellow Diamond Dove has pale yellow shoulders, back, wings, and tail while their head, neck, and breasts are light purple and their undersides are white. A bright red-orange eye ring encircles the ruby red eyes.

You do not *have* to show any of these dove varieties to own them, nor do you have to show your dove at all.

The brief descriptions above should, however, help you to appreciate the great diversity among the doves with which you can share your home.

Even in their wild state, doves are beautiful creatures, and enthusiasts, through selective breeding programs, have cultivated truly stunning color variations.

Chapter 2 – Are Doves the Right Birds for You?

There are always practical considerations about daily life, care, and husbandry to mull over prior to adopting any kind of companion animal. The following sections cover major issues associated with deciding on the suitability of doves as pets in your household.

Zebra Doves

Do Doves Get Along with Other Pets?

There's no getting around the fact that doves, by their very docile nature, are at the bottom of the food chain. They have no real ability to defend themselves against an attack and are only safe when housed in a strong cage secured against break-ins.

Do not place cages where they can be knocked over, even if

it means suspending the cage from a strong hook. A cage on a stand is only appropriate if well weighted. Cats are quite adept at scaling cages, and equally capable of using their clever paws to unlatch and open doors.

Never keep a bird of any kind in a home with a snake that is not completely secured. Be equally careful with ferrets. Remember, your dove has absolutely no ability to protect itself beyond flying away. Doves are prey animals. As cruel as it sounds, they are on the "menu" for many other species.

Do Doves Get Along with Other Birds?

Doves prefer the company of other doves or their own privacy. They have soft bills that are useless as a means of defense and their skin is extremely thin and fragile. Even a small parakeet can easily kill a dove.

When housed with other doves, it's important to be on the lookout for any sign of bullying. Males will fight during mating season and may need to be separated for their own safety. In general, as a beginner, your best option is to raise doves in mated pairs in a large, roomy cage.

A "mated" couple does not necessarily indicate a male/female combination. Doves often pair with their own gender, and a lone dove will even become attached to an inanimate object as its "mate."

If you do have a single dove, you will need to devote at least half an hour a day to holding and petting the bird to keep it from becoming depressed and lonely. Your doves will develop a bond with you even if they do have a partner, but for single doves, you are their mate.

Are Doves Suitable Pets for Children?

While doves are excellent pets for children due to the birds' gentle disposition, it is important that a child be supervised in caring for them. Doves will not survive rough handling.

Both the perches in the cage and the birds' feet must be kept clean to guard against infection. Doves cannot be startled or otherwise subjected to stress. They require fresh water at all times, and regular feeding. They must be supervised for signs of illness, and protected against injury.

Also, as a parent, you should realize that a dove in captivity could live as long as 20 years. Don't get one for your child unless you intend to take care of the bird for the duration of its life.

Should You Adopt a Male or Female?

In terms of gender selection, doves offer unique flexibility. Since the animals thrive in pairs, you can obviously keep a male and female, but you must be prepared for the birth of offspring and for their placement and care.

Doves form such close pair bonds, however, that male / male and female / female couples live happily together. This is not the case in many other species where males, especially, exhibit overt aggression toward one another.

Remember, however, that the birds pair for life regardless of gender. Separating a bonded pair is traumatic; a fact that you will witness clearly should one of your doves die. It is equally difficult to introduce a third bird. This is why paired population management is the best course of action.

The differences in behavior you will see with same gender dove pairs are slight. Female couples lay infertile eggs and engage in nesting behavior. With males there will be more bowing and cooing, which is their primary mating display.

How is a Dove's Gender Determined?

Adult doves, especially Ring Neck doves, show little if any gender differentiation. Females may be slightly smaller, but only by about 20%, which may not be readily apparent, especially to an inexperienced bird owner.

Diamond Doves have more sexual dimorphism. In terms of behavior, males will bow and coo, the two major aspects of the birds' mating ritual.

The most reliable method for determining gender, however, is a DNA test made by a veterinarian. If you buy your dove from a pet store, chances are quite good the employees at the store will have no more idea about the bird's gender than you do!

For this reason, I strongly recommend acquiring your dove(s) from a reputable breeder to secure the gender mix that will work best for you. Truly experienced dove keepers can often determine gender without a DNA test simply because they know the birds and their habits so well.

What Should I Know About Bringing Doves Home?

Doves are not "instant" pets. They are highly sensitive to stress. Everything your dove will need should be in place and waiting when you bring your bird(s) home. Don't buy a pair of doves as an impulse purchase!

Doves in transition should be placed in a quiet area with ample food and water and left alone to acclimate to their new surroundings.

Do not think you can simply buy a pair of doves and all the necessary equipment and just throw everything together. If you have other birds in your home, the new arrivals should be kept strictly separate for three weeks.

Wash your hands both before and after handling any of your birds, and watch out for any of the signs of illness I will discuss in the health chapter.

Why is Temperature Especially Important?

Temperature regulation is extremely important for successfully keeping pet doves. Never subject your pet to direct sunlight. Doves overheat rapidly and without immediate access to shade can die in a matter of seconds.

By the same token, doves cannot tolerate chilly air and drafts. If possible, keep your birds in a separate room with the air conditioning ducts closed. (This will also help to keep the dust generated by the birds from circulating throughout your house.)

Never let the ambient temperature drop below 65 F / 18.3 C in the room where your doves are housed. If you must heat the room, select a sealed oil-filled portable heater. These units, which are inexpensive (around $40 / £25.42), heat evenly and do not create drafts.

What are the Basic Safety Precautions with Doves?

Later in this text I will discuss dove "proofing" your home, but I cannot emphasize strongly enough that you must never underestimate the potential of a tame bird escaping, especially if the dove is startled.

When a dove is frightened, its primary instinct is to fly. Their wings are powerful and their movements are fast and unpredictable. Even if you are able to restrain your pet, you may seriously injure the dove in doing so.

Never take your dove outside unless it is caged. Always keep your pet indoors in a cage or in an aviary. Some dove keepers do allow their pets free flight time in the house, but only in secure rooms from which all possible sources of danger have been removed. If you must transport your pet outside of the home, use a proper carrier.

A simple small animal carrier that costs less than $20 / £12.95 will suit your purposes and for single use trips, a cardboard carrier costing approximately $5 / £3.24 will work as well.

Should Doves Be Kept in An Aviary?

There is no doubt that birds kept in aviaries have greater opportunities to exercise and to get fresh air and sunshine. There are, however, much greater husbandry responsibilities when keeping a flock of doves over having a pair.

First, there is the expense of building the aviary (including securing any permits and homeowners association approvals required in your area.) This includes selecting the correct materials to ensure that your birds are safe from predators.

Second, you will have to clean up every day after multiple birds and have an adequate means to dispose of the waste material. Birds create "dust" which is a combination of dander and dried feces.

The doves themselves are susceptible to a number of illnesses that stem from poorly maintained living conditions. Some of those maladies can be transmitted to humans. (See the chapter on health.)

Third, you will be a dove "dorm mother," in charge on monitoring interactions in your dove population and resolving instances of bullying – which can mean the need to segregate some members of the flock from the general population.

For many enthusiasts this level of keeping doves is the great joy of the fancy. This is certainly true for pigeon keepers that enter their birds in competitive races and maintain lofts with numerous inhabitants.

If you are a beginner, which is the level of enthusiast to which I am primarily speaking, I recommend starting with a single mated pair of doves. As you become more skilled in their care and really experience life with these beautiful creatures, you can decide to what level you'd like to take your hobby.

Many overly enthusiastic new owners start with multiple birds and full-blown aviaries only to find themselves completely overwhelmed by the responsibility and then overwhelmed by remorse when their birds sicken and die.

If you tire of your doves or realize you've gotten in over your head, do not turn the doves loose assuming they will survive on their own. Doves born and raised in captivity will starve in the wild or quickly fall victim to predators.

For your sake and for that of your doves, start slow. There's *always* room for expansion – and it's quite common for dove owners to wind up with multiple pairs that have access to some type of aviary enclosure.

What Are the Pros and Cons of Dove Ownership?

It's always a little daunting to discuss pros and cons of any companion animal. What sounds like the absolute perfect pet to one person might be another's nightmare.
Your best bet is to learn as much as you can about life with the animal you're considering *in advance of an adoption!*

You should never adopt any animal on the spur of the moment without truly considering not just your own needs but also those of your future pet.

- Doves need your companionship. If you don't have time to spend with your bird, don't get a dove.

- Doves need to be guarded against stress. If you're not willing to regulate your environment in your bird's best interest, don't get a dove.

- Doves are at their healthiest when they live in

pristine conditions. If you're not willing to clean your bird's cage daily, don't get a dove.

- Doves live as long as 20 years. If you are not willing to care for a pet for that length of time, don't get a dove.

Doves spend a great deal of time sitting happily in their cages. They don't do "tricks" or play with toys, but they are interesting intelligent creatures.

If you've never owned a bird of any kind, spend some time talking to someone who has actually lived with a dove. The Internet is an excellent resource to make contact with dove enthusiasts.

Don't make your decision until you're sure that this is the right animal for you. No list of "pros" and "cons" will be specific to your life circumstances and living conditions. Don't just think about yourself; think about the welfare of the animal that will rely on you for *everything*.

How Much Do Doves Cost?

The price of companion doves will vary greatly by source. Diamond Doves typically cost $45-$50 / £30-£32 each with some discounted pricing when purchasing a pair. Ring Neck Doves can be as much as $75 / £49 a pair.

Shipping Birds by Mail

Because doves are considered to be poultry, many of the

outlets for purchase you will find online deliver the birds to you via postal mail. I have listed some sources to buy doves at the back of the book. All were in operation when this text was written in the summer of 2015.

In the United States, the post office has approved boxes for mailing live poultry and postmasters are accustomed to handling the birds. Be aware, however, that unlike baby chicks, doves tend to sit quietly in the container during shipment.

Don't be alarmed if you go to the post office to get the package only to be told by a worried postal worker that the doves have shown no sign of life.

After you place your order, carefully track the progress of the shipment and retrieve the doves from the post office as quickly as possible. Although food and water is placed in the box prior to shipment, the sooner the doves are settled in their new home the better.

Only open the container in a secured room!

Before you purchase doves online from any source, carefully read the outlet's shipping policy. Don't hesitate to ask questions so you know exactly how the animals will be handled and how you should care for the doves once they arrive.

Chapter 3 – Dove Behavior

Doves are hardly the "action heroes" of the bird world, but they still engage in incredibly compelling behaviors.

- Doves are so loving as parents and completely family oriented that as the time for eggs to hatch nears, both parents will try to sit on the nest at one time.

- Even though mated doves have one another, they also have a real craving for the companionship of their humans. Their capacity for love and affection is that great.

- If you keep a single dove, the bird will bond completely to you. You are not just responsible for your pet's physical requirements in terms of food and shelter, but also for meeting its emotional needs.

- If you are not home during the day, you really should get a companion for your bird. Why? Because when a dove is lonely, it becomes depressed and suffers real emotional pain.

The more you can learn about your bird's needs on both the physical and emotional level, the better you will care for your pet. Remember, the longer you live with your dove, the better you will know what is normal for your bird.

Every dove is an individual, and behavior and environment are intimately linked. There's a great difference between a dove that is sick and one that is just annoyed because you moved its cage or changed something in the room.

Never think that you are being a worried dove "mother" or an alarmist. If you think that something is wrong with your dove that alone is reason enough to have the bird's health evaluated by a veterinarian.

Birds can sicken rapidly and die if they do not receive proper medical attention. Learning your dove's normal behavior not only allows you to bond more effectively with your pet, it also makes *you* the bird's primary healthcare "insurance."

The following tips and observations on behavior will help

you to create a supportive environment for your dove, and to better understand what your bird may be trying to "say."

Dove Communication

Although it is recommended that owners learn their birds' "language" and coo back at them in the name of companionship, it will soon be quiet clear to you that your dove regards you as rather slow in the communication department!

In order to get your attention so you can resolve whatever is bothering the bird, your doves may resort to a level of communication they think you are more suited to understand. For instance, a dove trying to get his point across:

- bang around in the cage
- flap from perch to perch
- rattle his seed cup
- do anything else to be noisy and noticeable

This may be the dove's way of saying he's hungry, his water needs changing, he wants more nesting material, or he's feeling neglected.

People often say they wish their pets could speak English because it would be so much easier to know exactly what the animal wants or needs instead of trying to guess. Imagine the dove's frustration! There he is, "speaking" perfectly coherent "dove" to a thickheaded human who is just not getting the message!

Dove Sounds

Remember that all doves are individuals and each one will have a unique vocabulary. That being said, these are some of the sounds you are most likely to hear.

- *Bow and Coo* – This is a combination action and sound. The dove bows deep and coos either to signal that another dove is trespassing on his territory or as an enticement to a female at breeding. The action may be preceded by a "laugh."

- *Laugh* – A chuckling sound that can be a territorial warning, an acknowledgement of successful mating, or a greeting upon returning to the perch. (Some enthusiasts refer to the "return" sound as a soft "giggle.")

- *Surrender* – A sound very like a whine that is an indication of non-hostile surrender, as in establishing a friendship. It can also be used by a mother dove to call her young, or as a signal of approaching danger.

- *Bark* – An indignant sound that expresses displeasure or dislike accompanied by a very disgusted expression, usually with the dove looking down its beak.

- *Scolding* – Used by female doves in a protective mode either for their home or nest and especially when guarding eggs or babies. A series of squeals with whistling and huffing.

- *Territorial Coos* – This is a male behavior that most often occurs at sunrise and sunset and can go on for an extended period of time. A male generally stands at a 45-degree angle while cooing, with the throat area ballooning outward. This is a signal of ownership and will especially be displayed when other males are near.

- *Twitter* – A kind of chattering sound not unlike that made by a chipmunk. It is generally a vocalization made as a warning or when the bird is straining, for instance if the animal is constipated.

Very young doves also peep, which can best be described as a long series of short, fast, high-pitched vocalizations, often to indicate distress. This may signal anxiety over locating the parent or signal that the baby is hungery.

Dove Actions

The same way that doves exhibit a range of predictable vocabulary, there are also common body movements. These include, but are not limited to:

- *Yawn* – Rather than signaling fatigue, a yawn is used by the dove to release air from the crop or by babies in anticipation of a feeding.

- *"Quiet" Talk* – You may see two doves moving their mouths without making sounds as if they are whispering to one another. This is a friendly gesture and is a type of introduction. Males and females with eggs or young offspring also use this behavior as a means to communicate without revealing the location of their nest.

- *Nuzzling* – This is a very frequent behavior that is a sign of affection. Nuzzling can also a precursor to billing and mating.

- *Wing Wobble* – A kind of flirtation or beckoning used in several ways: when a baby is hungry, when a female is billing with her mate, or when a nesting female is trying to get her mate's attention to bring her more nest material.

- **Billing** – Billing is foreplay between two doves in which the female entices the male to open his mouth so she can insert her bill deep into his throat. Generally followed by mating.

- *Driving* – When a male dove pecks his mate often because another male is present. There may also be warning laughs and bowing and cooing. Driving can become quite violent to the point of being abusive. It is an expression of ownership and control.

- *Preening* – The dove carefully uses its bill to arrange its feathers, passing them through the mandible. Similar to the manner in which one cat will groom another, doves will also preen for their mates, reaching places the bird itself cannot. Ruffling and shaking often follow preening.

Doves Dislike Changes to Their Environment

Doves do not like being moved from one home to another nor do they enjoy having their cage relocated inside the house — or even having the furniture near the cage changed. Choose your first location for your cage well!

Doves Like Routine

Doves like routine and do not like it when you do things "out of order." It's common for doves to show their impatience and displeasure by pacing back and forth in their cage as if to say, "I'm waiting!"

"Routine" extends to waking and sleeping schedules. Your doves will expect the lights to come on and go off at the same time each day and will basically tell you when it's time to "go to bed."

Fortunately, the birds are quiet animals and won't wake you up in the morning. If you're late, however, don't be surprised if your pet(s) are cranky. Just be thankful that unlike a rooster, your doves will never rouse you with a raucous crow!

Don't think you can do something just once or twice with a dove and then not repeat the action.

If, for instance, you give your pet a special treat at the same time 2 or 3 days in a row and then run out of the item, your dove will already have made the treat part of the perceived routine and be looking for it right on schedule.

Bonding Behavior

The best indication that a single bird has bonded with you is if the dove shakes its wings when you approach the cage and rewards you with a series of rapid light pecks on the fingers. That's your bird's way of kissing you.

If the bird is a male, do not be surprised if he bows and coos to you as if instigating the mating ritual. Males may even try to mount your fist if given the opportunity.

Bonded females are sufficiently stimulated to begin laying eggs and thus should always be given nesting material and a nesting box.

The little hen will sit on her eggs for the full 14 days even though they are infertile, at which time you should remove the eggs.

This allows the female's body to rest and to rebuild its stores of calcium before she lays a new clutch. Typically bonded females will lay eggs about once every three weeks.

Bonded male doves not only become affectionate, but have been known to defend their human "mates." Bonded females are quieter and more openly affectionate.

Be patient, the bonding process can take up to six months, but it will then last for the duration of the bird's life so long as you actively cultivate the relationship. Expect your dove to greet you with a happy coo in the morning and to want a little "hug" to start the day.

Sources of Agitation

When visitors enter the room, your doves may become agitated unless you stand near the cage. Ask people who come into your home that will be near your birds not to speak loudly or to make sudden movements.

Over time, your pet will become accustomed to people who are in your home on a regular basis.

You may even agitate your pet if you come close to the cage dressed in clothing outside your usual mode of dress or if you are wearing dark glasses or a hat.

Doves often do not react well to extremely bright colored clothing like pinks, reds, yellows, or stark whites.

Both dogs and cats will frighten companion doves.

Although dogs may ignore the birds while they are in their cage, Fido will go on the attack should the dove gets loose. Loud barking is also frightening to doves.

Frankly, as much as I like cats, there is no trusting one around a companion bird of any kind. It's a cat / bird instinctive animosity with a long history and not one you can expect either party to simply lay aside.

Don't take the risk! Fluffy sees your dove as one thing and one thing only – a snack.

Because a dove's skin is very thin and fragile, an attack by a cat is almost always fatal even if you are successful in getting the cat to turn loose of the dove. If actual physical wounds don't kill the bird, the stress of the attack will likely be fatal.

Night Frights

Use a night light in the room where your birds sleep so they can see their surroundings. A 40-watt bulb on the far side of the room is quite effective.

If a dove wakes up in a completely dark room and has been startled awake by a noise or movement they cannot identify, they will try to fly upwards, crashing into the cage. This often leads to broken wing feathers and bloody head wounds.

Special Section - Dove Releases

Dove releases at special events, especially "peace" themed events, have been popular for many years. Unfortunately, there has been little thought to the fate of the white doves that are the favored symbols for such displays.

White Ring Neck doves do not just simply fly off and survive. They are not equipped for life in the wild. Most starve slowly if they are not hit by automobiles or killed by other animals first.

These birds are cage bred to live as *pets,* not to care for themselves in a hardscrabble natural setting.

Companies that specialize in "dove" releases actually use white homing pigeons that are trained to return to their lofts at a distance of as much as 600 miles / 966 km. The average cost per a 12-bird release is about $250 / £163.

The American White Dove Release Association's voluntary standard for the release of white homing pigeons standing in as "doves" calls for the event to be held outside on a clear day and at an hour that gives the birds adequate time to return to their loft.

(See the end of this section for the entire text of the release standard.)

Unfortunately, there are few if any laws in the United States addressing the abandonment of birds raised for domesticated living. Therefore, it's legal to walk into a pet store, buy a White Ring Neck Dove, and go straight outside and release the bird.

While the symbolism of a white dove flying skyward at a wedding or funeral might be quite lovely, you are signing the bird's death warrant.

Unless you can work with a company that offers birds safely trained to be released and return to their home loft, do not support the release of white doves.

White Dove Release Standards of the American White Dove Release Association

- We love and take excellent care of our white doves.

- We release only trained white homing pigeons

outdoors during daylight hours.

- We release our doves within 50 miles from their home loft so that they can arrive home safely the same day.

- We carry our white homing pigeons in safe and comfortable, well-ventilated white wicker baskets, training baskets or pet carriers that provide adequate ventilation.

- We dress appropriately and arrive early to each event to conduct or supervise the dove release.

- We DO NOT release our doves at night or in inclement weather or rainstorms for the safety of the birds.

- We DO NOT release white ring neck doves, white squab, or untrained white homing pigeons for their safety and the dignity of your event.

- We DO NOT provide white ring neck doves, white squab, or trained or untrained white homing pigeons for-self release. Our dove releases require a trained and knowledgeable dove release handler for the safety of the birds and to ensure the dignity of the event.

- We DO NOT discriminate anyone on the basis of race, religion, national origin, gender, sexual orientation, or disability.

Source: American White Dove Release Association at: https://sites.google.com/site/awdahomepage/Home/white-dove-release-standards

Chapter 4 - Welcoming A Dove Into Your Home

After reading the last two chapters you should have an understanding of some of the factors that must be considered prior to adopting your dove. If you have any reservations about what is required to care for a dove and to interact with the bird daily, reconsider your adoption.

Are Doves the Right Birds for You?

To reiterate some key points:

- If there is one quality that a pet dove values in his or her human, it's constancy. These highly intelligent creatures are keen observers of their environment and of their human mates.

- Even bonded pairs will expect the kind of solid routine that makes them feel safe and secure in the world. Any human who is a creature of habit will completely understand this natural instinct in a dove.

- Although doves are not as fragile as popular perception makes them out to be, they do need to be guarded against stressors in their environment and they do need the companionship of their humans.

- Remember that with a lifespan of as much as 20 years, bringing a dove into your life is no minor commitment.

- If you cannot provide a safe and stable home for a companion dove and cannot spend the time your pet needs to bond with you and to have its emotional needs met, this is not the right bird species for you.

Just because doves are placid creatures that spend a lot of time happily sitting in their cages, do not make the mistake of believing that you can simply ignore these sensitive creatures.

A companion dove needs a great deal more from you than just food and water. It needs a real *relationship*.

Cage Selection

The cage you pick for your doves must be large enough that the bird can spread its wings fully on both the horizontal and vertical plane.

This is especially important if you plan to mate your birds since the male will need adequate space to fully flap his wings to ensure successful positioning for fertilization.

Ample room is also crucial for adequate exercise. Ideally, the birds should be able to hover inside their living space.

The cage for a single dove should be no smaller than 24" wide x 24" deep x 24" high / 60.96 cm x 60.96 cm x 60.96 cm. In any cage, make sure that you allow for a minimum of 10 inches / 25.4 cm above the flat perch.

Obviously if you are going to keep a mated pair of birds, double your calculations for cage size.

Some owners select cages that are specified for Cockatiels to get sufficient room for two doves. Any cage that is designated as a "flight" enclosure should be appropriate.

As an example, a typical flight cage "aviary" measures:

- 37.25" long x 27.25" wide x 49" high
- (94.61 cm x 69.21 cm x 124.46 cm)

The cost for the unit is approximately $280 / £181.04.

Securing the Cage Door

In shopping for a cage, select a unit with a hinged door that will not come open should the cage be knocked over.

Small luggage locks can also be used to further secure the door. Snap hooks are a good precautionary option as well. (If you do have other animals in the home, putting some type of lock on the dove cage door is a good idea.)

Doves Like Perches, Not Toys

Unlike parakeets and other companion birds, doves are not interested in toys or swings. They are relatively sedentary animals that spend the bulk of their time on their perches.

Doves do require a flat, stable surface with a width of approximately 2 inches / 5.08 cm where they will sleep. Many people use a plain, untreated "2 x 4" board attached to the sides of the cage with brackets that are readily available from large pet retail outlets like drsfostersmith.com.

Also provide a round perch no smaller than .5 inches / 1.27 cm or larger than .75 inches / 1.9 cm, which will help your doves exercise their feet. Consider adding a .75 inch / 1.9 cm cloth rope perch for the same purpose.

Time Out of the Cage?

If you have no other animals in the house and you can remove the dangers from a controlled and closed area, you can let your doves have free time out of the cage.

Some major potential hazards to remove or secure include:

- any open source of water like a toilet or full sink

- pretty much everything in the kitchen
- glass windows that are not covered*
- uncovered mirrors*
- anything fragile that can be knocked over and shattered
- portable heaters and open fireplaces
- ceiling fans
- household poisons
- areas behind furniture or appliances where your bird could become trapped
- open doors

* Your doves will not have the judgment to discern that a window or a mirror is a solid object and may try to fly through, or they may see their own reflection and try to engage with the other "bird," especially as a territorial defense.

Necessary Cage Accessories

Your dove's cage will need the following basic accessories. (The list includes grit and feed, which will be described in detail in the following section on diet and nutrition.)

- 1-2 seed cups priced from $3-$5 / £1.95-£3.26 each
- 1-2 grit cups priced from $3-$5 / £1.95-£3.26 each
- open water dishes at least 1" / 2.54 cm deep (not bottles) $3-$5 / £1.95-£3.26 each*
- round perches (number as spaces allows) $7-$10 / £4.56-£6.52 each
- flat perch (can be a simple 2 x 4) attached to cage sides with brackets $20 / £13.03

- nest cup $5-$10 / £3.26-£6.52
- nesting material $2-$5 / £1.30-£3.26
- bathing dish (2" deep) $5-$10 / £3.26-£6.52
- millet clip / holder $2-$5 / £1.30-£3.26
- millet (foraging treat) $3-$5/ £1.95-£3.26
- calcium grit $3-$7/ £1.95-£4.56
- fortified seed mix $5-$10 / £3.26-£6.52

* Keep water dishes on the small side or your doves will try to bathe in the "pool." A depth of 1" / 2.54 cm minimum is recommended as doves drink by placing their bill straight down almost as if they're drinking out of a straw. Monitor the quality of the water and make sure it is fresh and clean at all times.

Estimated total (excluding cost of birds and cage): $61-$97 / £39.73-£63.18

Costs for nesting material, millet, grit, and seed will be ongoing, with other accessories requiring replacement from time to time.

Bathing Dish

Your doves will enjoy their bath water more if you fill the dish with toasty warm water at least once a day. A dove's normal temperature is 103-106 F / 39.4-41.1 C, so lukewarm-warm water will feel cold to the bird.

Run the water to the temperature at which you would take a bath and your doves will be quite happy.

Diet and Nutrition

Because doves have soft bills, they cannot crack hard shells. For this reason, doves are especially fond of:

- millet
- oats
- milo
- raw shelled peanuts
- shelled sunflower seeds

Many of the dove mixes available in pet stores are actually formulated for wild doves and do not contain the necessary nutrition for captive doves. Always be sure you are buying a "dove and pigeon" food that is listed as "fortified."

- Expect to pay approximately $5 / £3.26 per 5 lbs. / 2.27 kg.

Vitamin Supplementation

Again, a dove's soft bill prevents it from using a mineral block or cuttlebone, so vitamin supplementation has to come in the form of a liquid added to the drinking water or as a powder mixed into their seed.

- There are many products available in this genre in a price range of $2-$10 / £1.30-£6.52.

Many dove keepers find that if they give their pets greens and fruits once or twice a week, vitamin supplementation is not necessary.

Millet

Doves do love millet, so keep a spray of millet clipped to the side of the cage as a nibble "treat."

- You will pay approximately $4 / £2.61 for 1 lb. / 0.45 kg of golden millet sprays.

Grit

Provide high calcium grit such as crushed oyster shell for your doves in a separate dish, not mixed in the seed.

- Calcium grit for birds sells for approximately $4 / £2.61 per 20 ounces / 567 grams. (Be sure the product you are buying is finely ground.)

Fresh Treats

A couple of times per week give your birds a special "salad" treat of chopped greens and fruit. A good mix would be spinach, apples, carrots, and melon.

(Always wash fruits and vegetables or buy organic.)

Place the fresh treat in a dish separate from the seeds and remove any uneaten bits in 24 hours.

Cage Maintenance

When you handle your doves, get into the habit of washing your hands before and after with an antibacterial soap for your own safety as well as that of your doves.

All portions of your dove's habitat should be kept clean and free of all traces of droppings. Use an antibacterial cleaner that is rated safe for use with pet enclosures.

Some products you may want to consider include:

- Healthy Habit Natural Enzyme Bird Cage Cleaner $12 / £7.82 per 24 fl. oz. / 710 ml
- Nature's Miracle Cage Cleaner for Birds $8 / £5.21 per 24 fl. oz. / 710 ml
- Poop-Off Anywhere Wet Wipes $10 / £6.52 per set of 70
- Natural Chemistry Healthy Habitat $32 / £20.85 per gallon / 3.78 liters

Always allow perches and other cage surfaces to dry completely before you put your doves back in their enclosure.

(While you are cleaning the main cage, house your doves in their travel box for their safety.)

Keep the bottom of the cage clean of all debris. Doves are grazers by nature. If they scatter their seed amid droppings on the floor of the cage, they will ingest their own excrement and that of their cage mates, which is a major vector of disease transmission.

Wash food and water dishes every day ensuring that no film or slime is allowed to accumulate. Soak and clean plastic nest boxes at least once a month.

If you are not prepared to clean your dove's cage *daily* do not adopt the birds!

Chapter 5 – Your Dove's Health

Due to their wide dispersal around the globe, doves can thrive in almost any climate. Although they are susceptible to stresses in captivity, the birds are not as fragile as they may appear.

Sound husbandry practices and preventive care measures are key to keeping a healthy companion dove.

Finding an Avian Veterinarian

When you work with a small animal veterinarian you are talking to a doctor whose primary experience is with dogs and cats.

Even highly qualified vets are often drawn up short by the health needs and even the anatomy of a companion bird.

If possible, it is to your benefit to find an avian veterinarian. You can begin your search at the home page of either:

- Association of Avian Veterinarians (www.aav.org)
- Federation of Aviculture (www.afa.birds.org)

In Europe, consult the European Association of Avian Veterinarians (EAAVonline.org).

Meeting the Vet for the First Time

Always schedule an office visit to meet the doctor without taking your dove along. Too often a pet owner's initial introduction to a veterinarian occurs in the middle of a crisis situation.

A better scenario for all concerned it to make sure, in advance, that you are comfortable with both the doctor's qualifications and personality.

Obviously in an emergency you simply want to get help for your pet, but the optimum situation is one that sets the foundation for a long-term healthcare relationship.

When you make the appointment, be clear that you are coming in to speak to the vet as a prospective client and that you are prepared to pay the full cost of an office visit.

Do not expect "freebies." That attitude will hardly get your relationship with the vet off to a good start!

Have your questions prepared in advance. Veterinarians are busy medical professionals. Don't waste their time. Some questions you may want to ask include:

- How long have you been treating birds and what type of birds do you see most often?

- Are you familiar with doves specifically and with their care?

- Do you have any birds of your own? If so, what type?

- Do you belong to any veterinary associations that

offer continuing education in avian care?

- Does this practice offer any options for emergency care outside your regular business hours? If not, where do you direct your clients to receive emergency services for their pets?

- May I have a schedule of fees and is there anything I need to know about how billing and payments are handled? Do you accept any type of pet insurance or have any recommendations in that regard?

- What is your recommended schedule for check-ups?

- Do you make house calls or are you open to house calls if the situation merits? If you do come to my home are your fees higher?

Although the idea of a "house call" seems antiquated, you will find that many avian vets actually will come to your home.

A bird that is seriously ill can be fatally stressed if taken out of its normal environment. A knowledgeable avian specialist is aware of and sensitive to this fact.

If you cannot locate an avian vet, find a small animal vet who is willing to treat your bird *and* to consult with other doctors and/or specialists if necessary to determine the correct course of action.

In this type of interview, try to assess the doctor's level of interest in your animal apart from any fees that will be collected.

Typically, vets are people who love animals and are willing to go the extra mile to ensure any species receives the necessary level of care.

Become Self-Educated

The more time you take to learn about potential illnesses and health problems that can affect your dove, the better advocate you will be for your pet's health.

Do not be afraid to ask questions or to question a recommended treatment, especially when you are working with a veterinarian who does not specialize in avian care.

Since doves and pigeons are really the same birds, online communities offer a powerful resource to enthusiasts to discuss all aspects of the dove and pigeon fancy. Some examples that were extant in the summer of 2015 when this text was written include:

- *Pigeon-Talk* at www.pigeon.biz
- *BackYard Chickens* at www.backyardchickens.com
- *Yahoo!'s Pigeon Groups* at groups.yahoo.com/neo/dir/1600962426
- *Avian Nation* at www.aviannation.com
- *The Dovecote Spot* at www.thedovecostespot.com

(Websites and online communities come and go. There is no way to guarantee that these sites will still be operational when you are reading this book. If you find that they are not, use your favorite search engine and look for "dove and pigeon discussion groups" or "dove and pigeon forums.")

Although any community will respond to an emergency message, take the time to establish yourself in advance as part of the group. Other people in your life may not understand why you think your dove is the best pet *ever*, but other fanciers will certainly understand!

It's best to "lurk" in an online community for several days or a couple of weeks until you begin to get a sense of how the board operates and who the people are who form the group.

Assessing Your Bird's Daily Health

For the emotional health of your dove, you should handle your bird(s) at least 30 minutes a day. This is an excellent opportunity to feel your pet's body and to assess the bird's overall condition.

A bird that is healthy has well-developed muscles in the breast and back areas, with strong feathering over the entire body. There should be no spots where they feathers are missing or thin.

The skin around the eyes and beak should display even coloration and appear to be slightly powdery. If you see gray spots, yellow deposits, or mucous along the lining of the mouth or along the jaw, some form of illness may be present.

Also watch for signs of mites or other parasites, including excessive scratching behavior on the part of your pet. Doves that are feeling well are alert. Their eyes are intelligent and interested, but they convey an overall serenity, with no evidence of agitation or discomfort.

Look at your dove's feet to ensure that they are clean. Doves are particular about their feet and will only allow them to be dirty if they are in ill health.

Any time that you introduce a new dove into the enclosure, quarantine the animal for at least ten days to ensure that your existing birds are not introduced to illnesses or parasites.

Doves should not be stressed by over-handling. These animals are placid by nature. They don't like loud noises, especially those that occur suddenly and at irregular intervals.

Pick your doves up and pet them for half an hour at least once a day, but otherwise don't be constantly "fiddling" with your birds.

Pay Attention to the Poop

With all species of birds, the consistency, color, and odor of the droppings are good ways to judge the animal's general health. Excrement should be well formed, firm, and odor free with a greenish brown color.

Observe the feathers around the anus in the area called the "vent." This region of your bird's body should be clean and dry. If the droppings are slimy or wet, the dove's plumage will be soiled.

Doves Have Soft Bills

The words "bill" and "beak" are not interchangeable, although in the common vernacular the two words are routinely substituted for one another.

- A **beak** is hard tissue similar to horn and is found in birds like parrots. A beak can be filed without causing the bird pain and without instigating bleeding.

- A **bill**, however, is soft tissue Doves have bills that can be torn and will bleed if wounded. One reason why doves seem so much more expressive than other birds is because their soft bills are flexible.

Beaks grow back if damaged; bills do not. A dove's bill is sensitive to pain and will bleed. When the bill is wounded, it must be repaired with stitches and some degree of damage will be permanent.

Calcium Deficiency in Caged Doves

Doves' soft bills make them more susceptible to calcium deficiency than any other caged companion bird. The *cannot* use mineral blocks or cuttlebones.

Their bills are too soft. It is *essential* that your caged doves be given calcium grit, oyster shells, or calcium carbonate. Fortified seed alone *will not* supply adequate amounts of calcium.

Calcium supplementation can either be given as a finely ground dust mixed with the doves' seed or as a water additive.

Birds suffering from calcium deficiency will suffer from neurological problems, be highly susceptible to broken bones, and lay eggs with overly soft shells.

Selecting a Healthy Dove

When picking your doves, look for the following features:

- The dove's head should be well rounded and slightly flat on top. Birds with extremely small heads are often not as intelligent and may be prone to illness.

- The upper jaw of the bill should be larger than the lower jaw, but both should be well aligned and meet properly, with good positioning and a solid appearance.

- The bird's flesh should feel muscular and solid, indicating good body conformation.

- The dove's feathers should be completely intact with a hard "flat" appearance.

Specific Warning Signs of Illness

Any of the following are specific warning signs of potential illness:

- Sleeping to excess.
- Sleeping on the bottom of the cage rather than on the flat perch.
- Having a "fluffed up" appearance.
- Poor appetite or refusing to eat at all.
- Listless and disinterested behavior.
- An inability to stand or the appearance of being lame.
- Labored and difficult breathing.
- Discharge from the nostrils or eyes.

- Swelling of the eyes or cloudy eyes.
- A bubbling discharge at the mouth.
- Soiling in the area of the vent under the tail.
- Tail bobbing.
- A beak that is overgrown or that does not align properly.
- Any change in the color, consistency, or odor of the droppings.

Avian Illnesses

The following conditions are not necessarily specific to doves, but can be seen in many kinds of birds. Almost all can be prevented by excellent husbandry practices. A companion bird's cage must be cleaned *daily*.

There is probably nothing you can do for your doves that will protect their health more than housing them in a well-maintained, clean cage.

Salmonellosis

The deadly bacterial pathogen for Salmonellosis (*Paratyphus*) is inhaled from dust, ingested in food, passed on during mating, or in general contracted from a poorly maintained environment. A female dove can also pass the bacteria to her young during feeding.

Any dove that survives an infection will be a carrier for life and may appear to be completely healthy, only shedding the pathogen during periods of stress. Infected embryos typically die before hatching.

The clinical signs of acute salmonellosis are most clearly seen in the droppings, which take on a greenish cast and will be filled with mucous. Young birds exhibit regarded growth and all affected doves will become emaciated as the infection progresses.

As the joints thicken, the dove is unable to maintain its balance and will become increasingly lame, often with a twisting of the neck. If the infection is present during molting season, the cast off feathers will be bloody at one end.

Antibiotics are used to treat salmonellosis. Affected birds should be quarantined and healthy animals removed from the enclosure, which should be thoroughly cleaned and disinfected. Many owners find it more prudent to simply discard all equipment and start over.

Ornithosis

Many birds around the world, including doves and pigeons, are affected by infectious ornithosis transmitted via dust, food, or water contaminated with the microorganism *chlamydia psittaci* . The disease presents in one of two ways:

- In acute cases, juvenile doves will wheeze when breathing, suffer from conjunctivitis, and have diarrhea.

- Doves that survive the infection and reach

adulthood are chronic carriers, shedding the pathogen to other birds and potentially to humans.

To determine the presence of ornithosis, a veterinarian or physician must take a blood smear from a dead bird or run a fecal test on a sample collected from a living animal.

Other symptoms include:

- swollen eyelids with blindness in one eye and visible discharge
- discharge from the nose with slime in the throat and sneezing
- coughing and rattling respiratory sounds
- scratching at the head / beak indicating discomfort
- poor body condition and weight loss
- overall lethargy

Standard treatments for ornithosis are antibiotics like doxycycline and tetracycline.

Coccidiosis

Dove and pigeon flocks around the world can be affected by an intestinal infection called coccidiosis caused by the coccidia protozoa. Under normal conditions, birds develop immunity against infection by ingesting small quantities of the parasite, which lives in their small intestine and guards the bird's system against other intestinal invaders.

In young doves, however, if the protozoa multiples beyond normal levels and causes an acute infection, death usually follows quickly.

The bird will lose weight rapidly, but consume large amounts of water and pass green, slimy droppings filled with blood. Lethargy sets in and the dove appears to puff out.

The greatest danger is to doves kept in poorly maintained enclosures with high levels of humidity. Superior husbandry is the best protection against a potential outbreak.

Young Bird Sickness

Young Bird Sickness or Adeno-coli Syndrome is an aggressive e.coli outbreak triggered by adenovirus. Uncontrolled proliferation of the e.coli pathogen in the dove's normal gut flora enflames the intestines causing diarrhea and bleeding.

The e.coli enters the bloodstream and invades the vital organs setting off a cascade of systemic septicemia. When both the adenovirus and the e.coli are present, the dove will stop eating, lose weight, pass clear watering droppings, and exhibit vomiting.

There are no effective drugs for viral infections, so treatment can only address the secondary bacterial infection.

Death usually occurs in a week. The best protection against Young Bird Sickness is maintaining a clean cage environment and minimizing stress.

Hexamitiasis

Hexamitiasis is an intestinal disease caused by *Hexamia columae*. Affected birds pass bloody, loose feces, which causes the disease to spread.

The incubation period is brief, just 4-5 days. Sick birds become rapidly debilitated, losing weight and taking in large quantities of water.

Diagnosis is made by cloacal or intestinal swabs examined under a microscope. There is no effective vaccination or treatment, with many surviving birds become carriers.

Hexamitiasis is seen most often in the summer and autumn. The only intervention for afflicted birds is to address secondary infections, usually with chlortetracycline or oxytetracycline.

Candida

When white lesions appear on the dove's mouth and throat, the bird is likely suffering from candida, an overgrowth of yeast in the intestinal tract that has progressed to the level of an infection.

Symptoms include lost off appetite and vomiting, with abnormally slow emptying of the crop. You will need to secure anti-fungal medication from your veterinarian to treat the condition.

Parasites

There are numerous internal and external parasites with which doves and all birds may become afflicted. The most common external parasites are mites, fleas, and lice.

All can be eliminated with a product like Harkers Duramitex Plus ($18 / £12 per 200 ML.)

Common internal parasites include tapeworms, hair worms, and round worms. All cause weight loss and a diminishment of physical conditioning. The bird's droppings will also become watery.

Commercial worming agents include such products as Combi-Worm, Belga-Wormac, Wormmix, and Worm-Ex.

Ingrown Feathers

During the later summer ever other year, your doves will molt. During this natural process, the bird will have bare spots on the body, but will never be completely "bald."

As new feathers come in some may become ingrown. Typically you will feel a red, inflamed lump on the bird's wing. Such lesions are filled with pus and will become an abscess if not properly removed.

Seek the assistance of a veterinarian to avoid the potential of infection and excessive bleeding.

What are Blood Feathers?

Blood feathers are the new feathers that come in when a bird molts. The new feather cannot grow without a supply of blood in the shaft. The largest blood feathers on any bird will be found in the wings and tail.

When the feather is fully grown, its follicle closes and the internal blood supply dries up. When these feathers break, there is no danger of blood loss to the bird, and the feather will remain broken until the bird molts again.

Chances are good that when a bird is not molting, it has no blood feathers at all.

Broken Blood Feathers

When feather that has a blood supply is broken, it can usually be treated at home with a small amount of styptic powder applied directly to the sound. If you have nothing else on hand, plain baking flour will serve the same purpose.

The Wing Clipping Debate

Frankly, I am a staunch advocate *against* clipping any companion bird's wings. The procedure is, in my opinion, barbaric and I do not believe the argument that mutilating a bird's wings to deprive it of its ability to fly is a way to keep your pet "safe."

Any bird will, when panicked, flap its wings and fly around, potentially crashing into objects and/or windows and harming itself. The solution, however is not crippling the bird!

Learn to appropriately handle your pet rather than subjecting it to a procedure that will not only take away its only means of escape, but will also permanently retard the development and growth of the bird's chest muscles.

Beyond what are, in my view, clear ethical concerns about wing clipping, if it is not handled correctly the dove will bleed to death.

Doves are placid, intelligent, loving animals. There is absolutely no need to subject such a creature to wing clipping. Cultivate a bond of trust with your pet and handling your dove will never be a problem.

Loss of Consciousness

All companion birds are highly sensitive to airborne toxins. If you discover your dove(s) unconscious, immediately remove the bird to another area oft he house and ventilate the room where your pet normally lives.

Do not house your doves near the kitchen or use any kind of cooking appliance or implement with a non-stick coating in close proximity to their cage. When such items overheat, they emit fumes that are deadly to companion birds.

Being Prepared to Render First Aid

Although it's not a good idea to try to treat any serious

emergency without the assistance of a veterinarian or a knowledgeable dove enthusiast, it is a good idea to have first aid supplies on hand. At the least, you should have:

- Antibiotic ointment for small wounds. Get a non-greasy formulation to prevent oil from getting on your dove's feathers and causing loss of body heat.
- Bandages, gauze, cotton balls, and cotton swabs.
- Small, clean towels in which to hold your bird.
- Pedialyte or a similar solution for use in reviving or supporting a weak bird.
- Styptic powder to stop bleeding.

It may be more convenient to purchase a pre-assembled avian first aid kit like those sold by Drs. Foster and Smith at www.drsfostersmith.com. A kit that contains the following costs approximately $22 / £14.26:

- one pair of latex gloves
- one 20 ml bottle of skin and eye wash
- 6 yards of 1" / 2.54 cm sterile gauze
- one pair of scissors
- one 5" pair of locking forceps
- iodine antiseptic swabs
- antiseptic towelettes
- 2" x 2" gauze pads / 5.08 cm x 5.08 cm
- roll of adhesive tape
- hand wipes for personal cleanup
- bird information emergency card to record veterinary information
- bird kit direction card

Never give your dove any medication intended for humans unless directed to do so by a veterinarian and then follow the instructions you receive to the letter. Many human medications are toxic to the companion birds and potentially deadly.

Chapter 6 – Breeding Doves

When you have a bonded pair of doves, they will remain a couple for life, protecting and defending one another and caring for each other lovingly.

As an example, some species of birds will kill another bird that is sick by attacking and pecking the weaker animal. Bonded doves are kind and compassionate, preening and nibbling at their partner to comfort and console it.

When one member of a bonded pair dies, the other mourns the loss, often plucking its own feathers as an expression of its grief and refusing to eat.

The bird must be provided with a new mate as soon as possible, and comforted by its human keeper in the interim, and even then the grieving period can continue until the bond with the new mate has been solidified.

Due to the strength of this emotional component in dove-to-dove relationships think carefully before allowing your pets to breed and to hatch eggs.

While it might be an interesting and even entertaining experience for you to watch your dove hen sit on and hatch out eggs and then feed and care for her young, to the doves, family is serious business.

There are also hard and practical facts that must be considered. It is more difficult to give away baby birds than it would be a kitten or a puppy – and think about the shocking number of unwanted and homeless animals of both kinds!

Releasing the young doves into the wild is *not* an option. They will not survive. To turn them loose to fend for themselves is not only cruel, but a sure death sentence.

There are no "throw away" pets. If you allow your doves to breed, you are responsible for either keeping and caring for their offspring or placing them in good homes.

Before you decide to allow your doves to reproduce, discuss the ins and outs of breeding doves with a more experienced enthusiast online or in person – especially if you do not have access to an avian veterinarian. You will need an expert to call upon if you have questions or concerns as the baby birds grow.

Nesting and Rearing

Breeding doves is extremely easy – the birds pretty much take care of everything themselves!

Your job is to supply the couple with nesting material, which you can purchase at any pet supply company that carries bird supplies. The commercial material mixes are generally grass hay, coconut fibers, and moss.

Doves can be bred as early as 6 months of age, and typically lay 2 eggs (one of each gender) that will hatch after a 14-day incubation period.

Both parents care for the young and both feed the babies "crop milk," which consists of partially digested food and a curd-like substance produced in the adult bird's crop.

It is important to provide your doves with plenty of water during the period when they are rearing their young to aid in the production of the crop milk.
The young remain in the nest for approximately 4 weeks and typically begin to fledge (put on their feathers) at about 12 days of age.

Hens can lay a new clutch every six weeks, but to allow your birds to do so would be extremely unhealthy. The recommendation is that no more than 3-5 clutches be produced per year.

Removing the nest box and nesting material can help to discourage breeding, but the only way to completely ensure that your birds will not breed is to keep same gender pairs.

Afterword

Although doves are a ubiquitous symbol in many of the world's cultures, the reality of life with these birds is not as simple as the image of a peaceful white bird flying into the sky.

As I pointed out in the special section on white dove releases, doves bred in cages to live as companion animals are not hardy enough to survive on their own in the wild.

This does not mean, however, that the birds are so fragile as to be difficult to keep as companions. With proper husbandry and reasonable shielding from stressors, a well-cared-for dove can live as long as 20 years.

The two varieties of dove most often kept as pets, Ring Neck Doves and Diamond Doves, offer the would-be enthusiast a beautiful range of color options. Most people think only in terms of white doves or small gray doves only.

In Chapter 1, in an effort to help you to gain an appreciation for this variety, I have typed on a long list of descriptions of the color types of both Ring Neck and Diamond Doves. If you have the chance, attend a dove show in your area to see for yourself the unique color ranges.

All of this dispels my own initial reaction to the idea of keeping doves as pets — "My God, how boring." Doves are anything but boring. They are loyal, affectionate, expressive pets that bond deeply to one another in mated pairs and with their human keepers.

Doves talk to one another and to us with a unique vocabulary of sounds and actions that are augmented by the individual personality of each bird. While doves may not be tricksters or daredevils — in fact, they're quiet and fairly sedentary — that are lovingly interactive and extremely interesting.

My primary cautions to those considering a dove adoption are these:

- Doves have a lifespan of as much as 20 years. If you are not prepared to have the bird in your life long-term, don't adopt.

- Doves need daily interaction from their humans. They are happiest when kept in pairs, but they still need a relationship with their keepers. If you are gone all the time or don't want to give that kind of attention to a pet, don't adopt.

- Doves are healthiest when they are kept in immaculate cages that are cleaned daily. This is a safeguard both for their health and for yours as many bird diseases can be transmitted to humans. If you cannot commit to daily cleaning, do not adopt.

If, however, none of these cautions strike you as a hurdle and in fact sound like something you would enjoy doing, then you are a prime candidate for dove ownership.

Welcoming a dove into your home and life creates a unique opportunity to bond with and to come to understand a living being quite unlike ourselves in form and function, but with a remarkable emotional capacity for love and devotion.

Special Section: Where to Buy Doves

Sissy Bird Colony
www.sissysbirdcolony.com/Ring Neck-Doves-Sale.html

Acquiring Diamond Doves
www.diamonddove.info/bird02_Acquiring.htm

PetCo
www.petco.com/product/118335/Doves.aspx

Birds Now
www.birdsnow.com/dove.htm

Birds Express
www.birdsexpress.net/doves.html

Bird Trader
www.birdtrader.co.uk/Doves/A/pigeons-for-sale.php

John Fowler
www.flatratewebsites.com/sites/dovepage/buy/john-fowler/index.html

George Schutt
www.flatratewebsites.com/sites/dovepage/buy/george-schutt/index.html

Phil Schultz
www.flatratewebsites.com/sites/dovepage/buy/phil-schultz/index.html

James Kell

www.flatratewebsites.com/sites/dovepage/buy/james-kell/index.html

Stromberg's

www.strombergschickens.com/prod_detail_list/Doves

Relevant Websites

The American Dove Association
www.doveline.com

Basic Dove Care
dovepage.com/care/

Diamond Doves
www.diamonddove.info

Dove Care Sheet
www.petco.com/assets/caresheets/bird/Dove.pdf

Doves and Pigeons as Pets
www.petassure.com/newsletters/110109newsletter/1101200
9article1.html

Dove and Pigeon Care
animal-
world.com/encyclo/birds/doves_pigeons/DovePigeonProfil
e.htm

Doves as Pets by Jeff Downing
www.birdchannel.com/bird-magazines/bird-talk/2010-
december/doves.aspx

The International Dove Society
www.internationaldovesociety.com

Mourning Dove
animal-world.com/encyclo/birds/doves_pigeons/mourningdove.php

Palomacy: Pigeon and Dove Adoptions

www.pigeonrescue.org

Pigeons and Doves - Feeding

www.vcahospitals.com/main/pet-health-
information/article/animal-health/pigeons-and-doves-
feeding/918

Raising Pet Doves

www.pet-doves.com

Ring Neck Dove

www.thatpetplace.com/Ring Neck-dove-article

Ring Neck Doves

www.parrotfeather.com/Ring Neckdoves/

Ring Neck Doves as Pets by Cathy Kendall

mickaboo.org/newsletter/jan12/art5.html

Glossary

A

air sacs - A system of nine interconnected sacs extend through a dove's body to circulate air.

arm - A dove's humerus, or arm, is the bone in the wing projecting directly away from the body.

aviary - An aviary is a wire enclosure designed to allow birds of any type greater freedom to fly and to move about than they would have in a conventional cage. Keep in mind that doves, which do better in mated pairs, may be subject to bullying in an aviary setting.

B

beak angle - The beak angle is formed between the beak and forehead.

billing - Billing is the action of a female dove reaching down a male's throat to receive an offering of regurgitated food. Often likened to kissing, the behavior is a precursor to mating.

bowing - Bowing is one of the courtship behaviors exhibited by a male dove, which includes puffing out the neck feathers, lowering the head, and turning in circles.

breast - The breast is the region of the body containing the pectoral muscles as well as the bird's crop.

C

canker – Canker is a disease of the mouth and throat that also affects respiration in pigeons.

clutch - A "clutch" is the complete set of eggs laid by a female dove.

cock – A cock is a male dove

condition - "Condition" refers to a dove's general health including the perfection of the feathers and muscle tone.

contagious – A contagious disease is one that can be transmitted from one pigeon to another.

cooing - "Cooing" is the sound that doves make during their courtship.

cover feathers - The cover feathers, which attach to the upper wing, comprise the greatest part of the wing surface.

coverts - The coverts are the small feathers of a dove's wings and tail.

crooked keel - A crooked keel is a deformed breast bone, which is considered a flaw in a doves.

crop - The crop is a bird's first stomach. Feed is stored in this fleshy pocket in the neck for up to 12 hours before passing on to the stomach and intestines.

D

dam - A dam is the female member of a mated pair of doves. Also referred to as a hen.

down - Down is the fuzzy body covering on a newly hatched pigeon.

droppings – Dropping are dove excrement.

E

egg-bound - When a dove hen cannot lay a fully formed egg, she is said to be egg-bound.

F

fancier – A fancier is a person who breeds doves or keeps them as companion or show birds.

flight – Flight refers to the 20 large feathers of a dove's wing. The 10 outer feathers are the primaries.

G

girth - Girth refers to the circumference of a dove's body.

H

hen - A hen is a female pigeon. Also referred to as a dam.

J

jewing - The jewing is the portion of the wattle located on the lower beak.

K

keel - The keel is the bone running down the middle of the breast. It is the point of attachment for the pectoral muscles.

keratin - Keratin is the protein that forms feathers.

L

mandible - The mandible is the beak or bill of a bird.

Mealy - A mealy is a light tan Racing Homer marked with red-brown bars across the back part of the wings' top surface

molt – Molting is the natural process of shedding feathers, which occurs in the late summer and early fall.

P

pectorals - The pectorals are the large muscles lying on both sides of the keel.

perch - The perch is an elevated place on which a dove sits. Round perches are used to help the birds exercise their feet, while flat perches provide a place for doves to sleep and to mate.

pin feather - A pin feather is a growing feather on young birds that has not yet broken through the shaft.

pipping - Pipping is the process by which young birds chip their way out of the egg shell during hatching.

plumage - Plumage is a bird's general feathering.

primaries - The primaries are the last ten large flight feathers on a pigeon's wing.

S

secondaries - The secondaries are the ten smaller flight feathers on the dove's wing lying next to the body.

sire - The sire is the male in a mated pair of doves. Also called the cock.

squab – A squab is a baby dove.

squeaker – A squeaker is a dove aged 2-8 weeks.

V

vent bones - The vent bones are two small bones located directly behind and on either side of the breast bone and under the tail.

W

wattle - The wattle is the fleshy covering of the nostrils

behind the upper beak.

Index

Feeding Baby
Cynthia Cherry
978-1941070000

Axolotl
Lolly Brown
978-0989658430

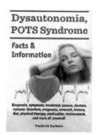

Dysautonomia, POTS
Syndrome
Frederick Earlstein
978-0989658485

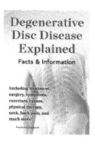

Degenerative Disc
Disease Explained
Frederick Earlstein
978-0989658485

Sinusitis, Hay Fever,
Allergic Rhinitis Explained
Frederick Earlstein
978-1941070024

Wicca
Riley Star
978-1941070130

Zombie Apocalypse
Rex Cutty
978-1941070154

Capybara
Lolly Brown
978-1941070062

Eels As Pets
Lolly Brown
978-1941070167

Scabies and Lice Explained
Frederick Earlstein
978-1941070017

Saltwater Fish As Pets
Lolly Brown
978-0989658461

Torticollis Explained
Frederick Earlstein
978-1941070055

Kennel Cough
Lolly Brown
978-0989658409

Physiotherapist, Physical
Therapist
Christopher Wright
978-0989658492

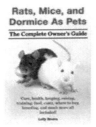

Rats, Mice, and Dormice
As Pets
Lolly Brown
978-1941070079

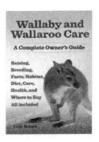

Wallaby and Wallaroo Care
Lolly Brown
978-1941070031

Bodybuilding Supplements
Explained
Jon Shelton
978-1941070239

Demonology
Riley Star
978-19401070314

Pigeon Racing
Lolly Brown
978-1941070307

Dwarf Hamster
Lolly Brown
978-1941070390

Cryptozoology
Rex Cutty
978-1941070406

Eye Strain
Frederick Earlstein
978-1941070369

Inez The Miniature Elephant
Asher Ray
978-1941070353

Vampire Apocalypse
Rex Cutty
978-1941070321

90111900R00066

Made in the USA
Lexington, KY
07 June 2018